1,000,000 Books

are available to read at

www.ForgottenBooks.com

Read online
Download PDF
Purchase in print

ISBN 978-0-364-03086-8
PIBN 11284956

1 MONTH OF
FREE
READING

at

www.ForgottenBooks.com

By purchasing this book you are eligible for one month membership to ForgottenBooks.com, giving you unlimited access to our entire collection of over 1,000,000 titles via our web site and mobile apps.

To claim your free month visit:

www.forgottenbooks.com/free1284956

English
Français
Deutsche
Italiano
Español
Português

www.forgottenbooks.com

Mythology Photography **Fiction**
Fishing Christianity **Art** Cooking
Essays Buddhism Freemasonry
Medicine **Biology** Music **Ancient**
Egypt Evolution Carpentry Physics
Dance Geology **Mathematics** Fitness
Shakespeare **Folklore** Yoga Marketing
Confidence Immortality Biographies
Poetry **Psychology** Witchcraft
Electronics Chemistry History **Law**
Accounting **Philosophy** Anthropology
Alchemy Drama Quantum Mechanics
Atheism Sexual Health **Ancient History**
Entrepreneurship Languages Sport
Paleontology Needlework Islam
Metaphysics Investment Archaeology
Parenting Statistics Criminology
Motivational

Historic, archived document

o not assume content reflects current
ientific knowledge, policies, or practic

ANNUAL WHOLESALE PRICE LIST
ALL 1924 - SPRING 1925

FRASER NURSERY COMPANY

(INCORPORATED)

HUNTSVILLE, ALABAMA

IT PAYS FNC TO PLANT

**FOR NURSERYMEN, FLORISTS, SEEDSMEN
AND DEALERS ONLY**

Fall 1924   Spring 1925

ANNUAL WHOLESALE PRICE LIST

OF THE

FRASER NURSERY COMPANY

(INCORPORATED)

HUNTSVILLE, ALABAMA

IT PAYS TO PLANT

IMPORTANT!

This list is intended to reach only those entitled to Wholesale Trade Prices. Errors are sometimes made, and in order that our mailing list may be corrected, we will thank any one in the trade to advise us should they have knowledge of our list reaching parties not so entitled.

For Nurserymen, Florists, Seedmen and Dealers Only

CUSTOMS OF THE 1

PRICES quoted herein are not good after April
to cancellation without notice any time unless

CASH or satisfactory reference, with sufficient ti
shipment, is invariably required of parties
sponsible, prompt paying parties, we will ext
ment.

REMITTANCES should be made by Draft on Ne
Louis, or by Express or Postal Money Order.

CLAIMS for damages or deficiencies to receive
made promptly upon receipt of goods.

RATES apply as follows: When 10 trees and 1
the price will be 2½ cents per tree more
Orders for 50 trees or more up to 300, whe
of each variety, will be charged at the pri
300 trees or more, when not less than 10 tr
be charged for at the price per 1000.

TELEGRAMS—Use Nurseryman's Telegraphic
will mail upon request. In connection with
word for each grade. When this cipher wor
or telegraphic orders no other description of

PACKING—We believe we excel others in the m
This is due largely to personal experience an
to insure contents from drying or freezing
ment be delayed in transit.

The cost of new boxes, well made, to be a

30x30x7½ to 10 feet	$4.00	18x24x7⅟
24x30x7½ to 10 feet	3.50	18x18x7⅟
24x24x7½ to 10 feet	3.00	15x15x7⅟

Bales 50 cents and up, according

SHIPMENTS—When ordering, please state pl
express shipment is desired, and give rout
absence of this information we will use ou
assuming any responsibility as to delivery.
risk and cost after delivery to the forwardi
Parcel Post system we are often able to
for less than the rates charged by the exp
desiring to secure the benefits of Parcel Pos
for postage in their remittances; the differ
funded promptly.

GUARANTEE—We are very careful to keep e
as labeled, and are ready at any time to 1
any that may prove otherwise, free of char
paid, but it is mutually agreed between the
that we shall at no time be liable for an
original purchase price.

CAUTION—All orders are accepted upon the
be void should any injury befall the stock
other causes beyond our control.

REFERENCES—Any Bank or Business House i
either of the Mercantile Agencies.

LONG DISTANCE TELEPHONE IN

FRUIT TREES

APPLE—One Year, Budded

	Cipher	Per
5 to 6 feet, whips	Gander	$25
4 to 5 feet, whips	Gang	20
3 to 4 feet, whips	Garb	15
2 to 3 feet, whips	Gash	12

Delicious	Yates
Early Harvest	Yellow Horse
Kinnaird	Yellow Transparent
Livland (Liveland Raspberry)	
Red June	Crabs
Stayman Winesap	Hyslop
Winesap	Transcendent

BARTLETT PEAR—Two Year, Budded on French

5 to 6 feet, 11/16 and up, well branched	Habit	50
5 to 6 feet, 5/8 to 11/16, well branched	Hail	40
4 to 5 feet, 9/16 to 5/8, well branched	Hair	35
3½ to 5 feet, 1/2 to 9/16, branched	Hall	30
3 to 4 feet, 7/16 to 1/2, mostly branched	Hand	25

KIEFFER PEAR—Two Year, Budded on Japan

6 to 8 feet, 1 inch and up, well branched	Health	40
5 to 6 feet, 11/16 to 1 inch, well branched	Hedge	35
5 to 6 feet, 5/8 to 11/16, well branched	Heel	25
4 to 5 feet, 9/16 to 5/8, well branched	Helmet	22
3½ to 5 feet, 1/2 to 9/16, branched	Hope	18

BARTLETT PEAR—One Year, Budded on Japan

5 to 6 feet, whips and few branches	Hopper	40
4 to 5 feet, whips and few branches	Hornet	30
3 to 4 feet, whips and few branches	Horse	25
2 to 3 feet, whips	Horrid	20

KIEFFER PEAR—One Year, Budded on Japan

5 to 6 feet, whips and few branches	House	25
4 to 5 feet, whips and few branches	Hovel	20
3 to 4 feet, whips and few branches	Hull	15
2 to 3 feet, whips	Hurt	10

SOUR CHERRY—Two Years, on Mahaleb

5 to 6 feet, 1 inch and up, well branched	Idol	60
5 to 6 feet, 11/16 to 1 inch, well branched	Ignore	50
4 to 6 feet, 5/8 to 11/16, well branched	Image	45
3½ to 5 feet, 9/16 to 5/8, well branched	Impair	40
3 to 5 feet, 1/2 to 9/16, well branched	Imply	30

Large Montmorency   Richmond (Early Richmond)

SWEET CHERRY—One Year, on Mahaleb

	Cipher	Per
5 to 6 feet, whips and branched	Impost	$50
4 to 5 feet, whips and branched	Impress	40
3 to 4 feet, mostly whips	Imprint	30

Black Tartarian   Governor Wood

SOUR CHERRY—One Year, on Mahaleb

3 to 4½ feet, 9/16 and up, well branched	Indorse	35
2½ to 3½ feet, 7/16 to 9/16, well branched	Indurate	25
2 to 3 feet, 5/16 to 7/16, well branched	Industry	17

Large Montmorency May Duke Richmond (Early Richmond)

PEACH—One Year

		Per 1
5 to 7 feet, 11/16 and up, well branched	Jaquar	$225
5 to 6 feet, 5/8 to 11/16, well branched	Javelin	22
4 to 5 feet, 9/16 to 5/8, well branched	Jersey	20
3½ to 5 feet, 1/2 to 9/16, well branched	Jewel	17
3 to 4 feet, 7/16 to 1/2, branched	Jobber	15
3 to 4 feet, under 7/16, whips and few branches	Join	12
2 to 3 feet, partly branched	Joy	10

Alexander	Greensboro
Arp Beauty	Heath Cling
Belle of Georgia	Hiley
Carman	J. H. Hale
Champion	Krummel
Chinese Cling	Mayflower
Crawford's Early	Rochester
Crawford's Late	Salway
Elberta	Wonderful
Fitzgerald	

APRICOT—One Year, on Apricot

		Per
5 to 6 feet, 5/8 to 11/16, well branched	Lace	$3
4 to 6 feet, 9/16 to 5/8, well branched	Lair	3
3½ to 5 feet, 1/2 to 9/16, branched	Lamp	2
3 to 4 feet, under 1/2, whips and branched	Lance	2
2 to 3 feet, mostly whips	Lap	1

Early Golden   Wilson
Royal

QUINCE—Two Year

3 to 4 feet, 7/16 to 1/2, well branched	Quart	4

Champion   Orange

PLUM—One Year, on Peach

	Cipher	Per 100
eet, 11/16 and up, well branched	Kick	$45.00
eet, 5/8 to 11/16, well branched	Kilt	35.00
eet, 9/16 to 5/8, well branched	Kink	30.00
feet, 1/2 to 9/16, branched	Kirk	25.00
eet, 7/16 to 1/2, branched	Kite	20.00
eet, under 7/16, whips and branched	Klick	15.00

ice   Wickson

                        Shropshire Damson

e

FIGS—One Year

feet, whips and branched	Fib	35.00
feet. whips and branched	Fiber	30.00
inches, whips	Finch	25.00

Turkey   Celestial

MULBERRY—One Year

et, whips	Muddy	30.00
et, whips	Mull	25.00
et, whips	Multiple	20.00
et, whips	Mush	15.00

ice (Barnes)   Hicks

n (New American)   Monarch

ç

JAPANESE PERSIMMON—One Year, Grafted

et, whips	Myriad	40.0
et, whips	Mystery	35.0

l   Triumph

e   Yemon

                Zengi

ishi

NUT TREES

S, Standard Varieties	Cipher	Per 10
5 feet	Peck	$70.0
4 feet	Pencil	60.0
3 feet	Pend	50.0

                Pabst

er   Schley

aker   Stuart

JT, English

5 feet	Waddle	75.0
4 feet	Wade	60.0
3 feet	Wag	50.0
24 inches	Wait	40.0
18 inches	Waive	25.0

WALNUT, Japan
    6 to 8 feet..
    5 to 6 feet..
    4 to 5 feet..
    3 to 4 feet..
    2 to 3 feet..

SMALL FRUIT

BLACKBERRY—One Year, No. 1..............................
Early Harvest   Mersereau
Eldorado   Snyder

DEWBERRY—One Year, Tips..............................
Austin   Lucretia

RASPBERRY—One Year, No. 1
    Cumberland (Black)..............................
    Cuthbert (Red)..............................
    Gregg (Black)..............................
    St. Regis (Everbearing)..............................
    St. Regis (Everbearing) Transplanted..........
CURRANTS—Two Year, Medium..............................
Cherry   Wilder

GOOSEBERRY—Two Year, Medium..............................
Downing   Houghton

GARDEN ROOT

ASPARAGUS—Two Year crowns, all standard
HORSE RADISH—Common, 6 to 8 inch sets......
RHUBARB—One Year, selected..............................
Linnaeus   Victoria

GRAPES

Two Year, No. 1

Campbell's Early..............................
Concord ....
Delaware ....
Diamond (Moore's Diamond)..............................
Ives ....
Lutie ....
Moore (Moore's Early)..............................
Niagara ....
Worden ....
Woodruff Red ....
James (Black Scuppernong) ....
Scuppernong (White) ....

VINES

LOPSIS tricuspidata veitchi (Boston Ivy)   Cipher
years, No. 1..Vicar

ATIS henryi, white, 2 years, No. 1...............Vicious
:kmanii, purple, 2 years, No. 1....................Victim
me. Edouard Andre, red, 2 years, No. 1........Victor
niculata, 2 years, No. 1................................View

RA helix (English Ivy)
years, No. 1 field grown............................Village
year, from 2½ inch pots............................Villian

ARIA thunbergiana (Kudzu Vine)
years, No. 1..Violin

PRIVET

;TRUM AMURENSE (Amour River Hardy) Cipher
  to 3 feet, 4 branches and up....................Prairie
  to 3 feet, 2 and 3 branches....................Prance
: to 24 inches, 4 branches and up................Prank
  to 24 inches, 2 and 3 branches..............Prate
  to 18 inches, 3 branches and up..............Prattle
: to 18 inches, 2 branches........................Prayer
  to 12 inches, 3 branches and up..............Preach

\
: to 3 feet, well branched........................Preamb
: to 24 inches, branched..........................Prebenc
: to 18 inches, branched..........................Precede

NICUM (Japanese Privet) (See Broad Leaved Evergr

,IFOLIUM (California Privet)
: to 3 feet, 4 branches and up....................Preecept
: to 3 feet, 2 and 3 branches....................Preciou
} to 24 inches, 4 branches and up................Precise
} to 24 inches, 2 and 3 branches................Preclud
: to 18 inches, 3 branches and up..............Predica
: to 18 inches, 2 branches........................Predict
: to 12 inches, 3 branches and up..............Preface
food transplanting grade, suitable also
   for grafting..Prefer

;LIANUM (Regels or Prostrate Privet)
} to 24 inches, well branched....................Prejudi
: to 18 inches, well branched....................Prelude

NSE (Amour River—Southern Type)
} to 4 feet, well branched........................Prelate
: to 3 feet, well branched........................Premiu:
} to 24 inches, well branched....................Prepare
: to 18 inches, branched..........................Prescril

YOUNG EVERGREENS

ORNAMENTAL TREES

Cipher   P

CORNUS florida rubra (Red Flowering Dogwood)

 2 to 3 feet..Object $
 18 to 24 inches...................................Oblige

MALUS ioensis bechteli (Bechtel's Double Flowering Cr:

 3 to 4 feet, well branched... ....Ob'ong
 2 to 3 feet, branched ....Obscure
 18 to 24 inches, branched ....Observe

MELIA azedarach umbraculiformis (Texas Umbrella)

 6 to 8 feet...Obtrude
 5 to 6 feet...Occasion
 4 to 5 feet...Occupy
 3 to 4 feet...Occur
 2 to 3 feet...Ocean

MIMOSA julibrissin (Acacia)

 3 to 4 feet, 2 year transplanted..........Octagon
 2 to 3 feet, 2 year transplanted..........Odd
 18 to 24 inches, 2 year transplanted....Offal

PRUNUS triloba (Double Flowering Plum)

 3 to 4 feet, well branched-----------------Offend
 2 to 3 feet, well branched-----------------Offset
 18 to 24 inches, branched ----------------Olden

JUNIPERUS PFITZERIANA

IFEROUS EVERGREENS

lude balling and burlapping where necessary.

IS (Retinospora) Japan Cypress

	Cipher	Per 10	Per 100
....Earl		$35.00	
₂S ....Earn		25.00	
₂S .... ·.................Earnst		20.00	
.... Earth		35.00	
.:..Earthly			$250.00
₂S ....:...........Earthquake			200.00
₂S ....Ease			150.00
₂S ....East			100.00
..:...Easter		35.00	
....Easy			250.00
₂S..Eaves			200.00
₂S...Ebb			150.00
₂S..:..Ebony			100.00

ι (Green)

	Cipher	Per 10	Per 100
₂S..Eccentric		25.00	
₂S..Echo			200.00
₂S..Eclipse			150.00
₂S..Economy			125.00
₂S..Effort			100.00

BIOTA AUREA NANA; JUNIPERUS VIRG. GI

CONIFEROUS EVERGREENS—(Co₁

CHAMAECYPARIS pisifera
squarrosa veitchi (Veitch's Silver Cypress) Cipher
- 30 to 36 inches...Either
- 24 to 30 inches...Elabora
- 18 to 24 inches...Elan
- 15 to 18 inches...Elapse
- 12 to 15 inches...Elect

JUNIPERUS chinensis pfitzeriana (Pfitzer's Chine
- 30 to 36 inches...Electio
- 24 to 30 inches...Elective
- 18 to 24 inches...Electrif
- 15 to 18 inches...Elegy

communis (Common Juniper)
- 30 to 36 inches...Elemen
- 24 to 30 inches...Elepha
- 18 to 24 inches...Elevato

communis hibernica (Irish Juniper)
- 18 to 24 inches, well filled.......................Elfin

excelsa stricta (Greek Juniper)
- 24 to 30 inches, well formed...................Elicit
- 18 to 24 inches, well formed...................Elite
- 15 to 18 inches, well formed...................Elixir
- 12 to 15 inches...Elk

JUNIPERUS virginiana (Red Cedar)
- 30 to 36 inches...Elm
- 24 to 30 inches...Elope
- 18 to 24 inches...Elude

CONIFEROUS EVERGREENS—(Continued)

JUNIPERUS virginiana

glauca (Virginia Blue Cedar)	Cipher	Per 10	Per
3 to 4 feet	Elusive	$45.00	
30 to 36 inches	Embark	35.00	
24 to 30 inches	Embassy		$300
18 to 24 inches	Embers		200

sabina tamariscifolia

24 to 30 inches, spread	Embody	30.00	
18 to 24 inches, spread	Emboss	25.00	
15 to 18 inches, spread	Embower	20.00	

PINUS montana mughus (Dwarf Mugho Pine)

18 to 24 inches, spread	Embrace	22.50	
15 to 18 inches, spread	Embroider	17.50	
12 to 15 inches, spread	Emerald	13.50	

THUYA occidentalis Tom Thumb

18 to 24 inches, spread	Emergency		200
15 to 18 inches, spread	Emery		150
12 to 15 inches, spread	Emigrate		125

occidentalis globosa (Globe Arborvitae)

18 to 24 inches	Emit		150
15 to 18 inches	Emotion		125
12 to 15 inches	Emperor		100

occidentalis hoveyi (Hovey's Golden Arborvitae)

18 to 24 inches	Emphasis		150
15 to 18 inches	Emphatic		125
12 to 15 inches	Empire		100

occidentalis pyramidalis (Pyramidal Arborvitae)

30 to 36 inches	Employ	20.00	
24 to 30 inches	Empower		150
18 to 24 inches	Empress		125
15 to 18 inches	Emulate		100

THUYA orientalis (Biota) (Chinese Arborvitae)

4 to 5 feet, selected well formed	Emulating		200
3 to 4 feet, selected well formed	Emulation		150
30 to 36 inches, well formed	Emulator		100
24 to 30 inches, well formed	Emulsion		75.
18 to 24 inches	Enact		50.

orientalis aurea conspicua

| 24 to 30 inches | Enamel | 25.00 | |
| 18 to 24 inches | Encamp | 20.00 | |

orientalis aurea nana (Berckman's Golden Arborvitae)

18 to 24 inches	Encroach		250.
15 to 18 inches	Encumber		175.
12 to 15 inches	Endanger		125.

TSUGA canadensis (Hemlock Spruce)

| 24 to 30 inches, well filled | Endorse | 22.50 | |
| 18 to 24 inches, well filled | Endow | 17.50 | |

PHOTINIA SERRULATA

BROAD LEAVED EVERGREENS

Prices include balling and burlapping where necessary

BELIA grandiflora (Rupestris)	Cipher	Per 10	Per 1(
2 to 3 feet, well branched..............Encourage			$ 40.(
18 to 24 inches, well branched..............Enchant			25.(
12 to 18 inches, well branched..............Encore			15.(

ZALEA hinodegiri

18 to 24 inches, with bloom buds..............Endure	$30.00
15 to 18 inches, with bloom buds..............Enemy	25.00
12 to 15 inches, with bloom buds..............Energy	20.00
10 to 12 inches, with bloom buds..............Enervate	15.00

UONYMUS japonica (Evergreen Euonymus)

| 24 to 30 inches, well branched..............Enforce | 90.(|
| 18 to 24 inches, well branched..............Engage | 65.(|

carrierei

24 to 30 inches, well branched..............Engine	45.(
18 to 24 inches, branched..............Engross	35.(
12 to 18 inches, branched..............Engulf	25.(

IGUSTRUM japonicum (Japanese Privet)

4 to 5 feet, well branched ....Enhance	100.(
3 to 4 feet, well branched ....Enliven	85.(
2 to 3 feet, well branched ....Enlist	60.(
2 to 3 feet, well branched, roots puddled ....Enormous	40.(

) LEAVED EVERGREENS—(Continued)

dum (Wax Leaf Privet)	Cipher	Per 10	Per 10(
es, well branched..............Enrobe			$150.00
es, well branched..............Enroll			125.00

aul Privet)
| es, well branched..............Ensnare | | | 125.0(|
| es, well branched..............Ensue | | | 100.0(|

ica (Holly Leaf Mahonia)
es....................:.......................Entail		$20.00	
es...................................Enter		15.00	
es..................................Entrap		12.50	
es..................................Entrust		10.00	

lata
well branched...................Envious			150.0(
es, well branched ....Envoy			125.0(
es, branched ....Envy			100.0(

DECIDUOUS SHRUBS

ALTHEA—Bush Form

Two Years

	Cipher	Per 10(
branched..............Sardonic		$25.0(
branched..............Satonic		17.5(
ell branched..............Satire		12.5(

)le violet.
a—large double red.
—very double, bright red.
ainaut—double, pinkish white.
nt—very double, dark red.
—double, pure white.
—semi-double, rosy white.
-very double, rosy pink.
ii plena—double purple.
: red.
ingle, pure white.
-single, pure white.

na alba (White Flowering Almond)
well branched..............Satisfy		60.0(
well branched..............Saucy		50.0
es, well branched..............Sausage		40.0

ik Flowering Almond)
| well branched...............Savage | | 50.0 |
| es, well branched..............Saving | | 40.0 |

CREPE MYRTLE

DECIDUOUS SHRUBS—(Conti

ERBERIS thunbergi (Japanese Barberry)
18 to 24 inches, well branched..............................
15 to 18 inches, well branched..............................
12 to 15 inches, well branched..............................

UDDLEIA davidii magnifica (Butterfly Bush)
2 years, No. 1..

lindleyana
2 years, No. 1..

ALYCANTHUS florida (Sweet Shrub)
2 to 3 feet, well branched..............................
18 to 24 inches, well branched.................. ....

ARYOPTERIS incana (Mastacanthus) Blue Spir
24 to 30 inches, well branched..............................
18 to 24 inches, well branched..............................

EUTZIA crenata and Pride of Rochester
3 to 4 feet, well branched..............................
2 to 3 feet, well branched..............................
18 to 24 inches ....
12 to 18 inches ....

XOCHORDA grandiflora (Pearl Bush)
3 to 4 feet, well branched..............................
2 to 3 feet, well branched..............................
18 to 24 inches ....

DECIDUOUS SHRUBS—(Continued)

A, Assorted   Cipher   Per

feet, well branched.............................Secure $

feet, well branched.............................Sedan

    Fortunei   Intermedia   Viridissima   Suspensa

EA arborescens grandiflora alba (Hills of Snow)

feet, well branched.............................Sedate

4 inches, well branched.........................Segment

ι grandiflora

feet, well branched.............................Seldom

4 inches, well branched.........................Select

ι grandiflora, Tree Form

feet, well branched.............................Selfish

ι (Oak Leaved Hydrangea)

feet, well branched.............................Senate

feet, well branched.............................Sensible

4 inches, well branched.........................Sentence

M moserianum (Gold Flower)

feet. heavy ....Sentinel

4 inches, well branched.........................Sentry

8 inches, branched ....Serge

ι humile (Nearly evergreen and everblooming)

s, well branched................................Serial

ι (Yellow Jasmine)

s. extra heavy ....Sermon

s, well branched ....Serpent

ιOEMIA indica (Crepe Myrtle)

feet, well branched.............................Servant

feet, well branched.............................Servile

4 inches, well branched.........................Settle

Lavender   Pink   Red   White   Crimson

Dwarf Crimson 10c. per plant extra.

, Assorted

feet, well branched.............................Shad

feet, well branched.............................Shaft

4 inches, well branched.........................Shallow

    Fragrantissima   Morrowi   Pink Tartarian

PHUS, Assorted

feet, well branched.............................Shamble

feet, well branched.............................Shame

4 inches ....Shark

    Coronarius   Lewisi (Gordonianus)

ιUS kerrioides (White Kerria)

feet, well branched.............................Shatter

4 inches, well branched.........................Shaver

SPIREA PRUNIFOLIA

DECIDUOUS SHRUBS—(Con

SPIREA bumalda Anthony Waterer
   24 to 30 inches, well branched............................
   18 to 24 inches, well branched............................
   15 to 18 inches, well branched............................

callosa rosea
   2 to 3 feet, well branched............................
   18 to 24 inches, well branched............................

prunifolia flore plena (Bridal Wreath)
   4 to 5 feet, well branched............................
   3 to 4 feet, well branched............................
   2 to 3 feet, well branched............................
   18 to 24 inches, well branched............................

reevesiana flore plena
   3 to 4 feet, well branched............................
   2 to 3 feet, well branched............................
   18 to 24 inches, well branched............................

thunbergi
   24 to 30 inches, well branched............................
   18 to 24 inches, well branched............................

van Houttei
   3 to 4 feet, well branched............................
   2 to 3 feet, well branched............................
   18 to 24 inches, well branched............................
   12 to 18 inches, branched............................

ASSORTED SHRUBS

DECIDUOUS SHRUBS—(Continued)

CARPOS racemosus (Snowberry)	Cipher	Per 100
feet, well branched	Shoot	$30.00
feet, well branched	Shop	20.00
4 inches, well branched	Shout	15.00

Red Snowberry or Indian Currant'.

) inches, well branched	Shovel	20.00
4 inches, well branched	Shower	15.00

hispida aestivalis

feet, well branched	Shrill	25.00
4 inches, well branched	Shrine	20.00

hendersonia

feet, well branched	Shroud	30.00
feet, well branched	Shuck	25.00

feet, well branched	Shudder	30.00
feet, well branched	Shuffle	25.00
4 inches, well branched	Shutter	18.00

ROSES

ROSES—Field Grown, Budded and On Own Roots

P.) Hybrid Perpetual, (H. W.) Hybrid Wichuriana, (H. C.) F
g, (Mtf.) Multiflora. (S.) Setigera, (C. P.) Climbing Polya
Climbing Tea and Ramblers, No. 1, graded 3 or more bra
inches in length; No. 2, graded 2 and 3 branches 18 to 24 i
h.

) Tea and (H. T.) Hybrid Tea, No. 1, graded 3 or more bra
inches in length; No. 2, graded 2 and 3 branches 12 to 18 i
h.
) Budded. (O. R.) Own Roots.

	No. 1 Per 100	N Pe
n Pillar—CP—large bunches of pink (O.R.)	$25.00	$
3rown—HT—creamy white (B)	35.00	
g American Beauty—HC—rich red (O.R.)	25.00	
F. Meyer—HR—bright pink (B)	30.00	
Rambler—rich crimson (O.R.)	25.00	
Perkins—HW—bright pink (O.R.)	20.00	
s of China—HC—bright red (O.R.)	20.00	
e Lyon—T—bright sulphur yellow (B)	35.00	
—HW—Red Dorothy Perkins (O.R)	20.00	

	No. 1 Per 100	N Per
Frau Karl Druschki—HP—pure white (B)	$30.00	$2
General Jacqueminot—HP—bright red (B)	30.00	2
Gruss an Teplitz—HT—fiery crimson (B)	35.00	'2
Heinrich Munch—HP—a true pink Druschki (B)	30.00	2
Hiawatha—HW—single crimson (O.R.)	25.00	1
Jonkherr J. L. Mock—HT—clear pink (B)	35.00	2
K. A. Victoria—HT—pure white (B)	35.00	2
Madam Plantier—HP—pure white (O.R.)	25.00	
Maman Cochet—T—rosy pink (B)	35.00	
Ophelia—HT—brilliant Salmon-flesh (B)	35.00	
Paul Neyron—HP—deep rose (B)	30.00	
Pink Roamer—HW—single pink (O.R.)	20.00	
President Taft—HT—deep pink (B)	35.00	
Queen of Prairie—S—rosy red (O.R.)	25.00	
Radiance—HT—brilliant rosy carmine (B)	35.00	
Red Radiance—HT—bright pure red (B)	35.00	
Red Letter Day—HT—glowing scarlet-crimson (B)	35.00	
Rhea Reid—HT—rich, velvety red (B)	35.00	
Seven Sisters—Mtf.—crimson to white (O.R.)	25.00	
Tausendschon—Rambler—deep pink (O.R.)	20.00	
Ulrich Brunner—HP—Hardy American Beauty (B)	30.00	
White Dorothy Perkins—HW (O.R.)	20.00	

HARDY PERENNIALS

	Per
Cannas, King Humbert, Yellow King Humbert and Eureka (White), strong roots	$
Coreopsis lanceolata grandiflora (Tickseed)	
Phlox, assorted varieties	
Tuberose, Excelsior Pearl	
Tuberose, Mexican	

LINING OUT STOCK

Per 10

Buxus sempervirens suffruticosa (Dwarf Box) 2 to 4 inches............$ 60

Deutzia crenata and Pride of Rochester, 18 to 24 inches................. 50.
   12 to 18 inches.. 35

Euonymus carrierei, 2 year transplanted.. 40

Jasminum nudiflorum, 2 year transplanted.. 45

Ligustrum amurense (Amour River Hardy Privet)
   1 year from open ground... 25
   rooted cuttings 15

  ovalifolium (California Privet)
   good transplanting grade.. 8

  sinense (Southern Evergreen Privet)
   1 year seedlings, 12 to 18 inches... 17
   6 to 12 inches... 10

Lonicera fragrantissima (Upright Fragrant Honeysuckle)
   1 year, 12 to 18 inches.. 50
   6 to 12 inches... 35

Mimosa julibrissin (Acacia) 1 year seedlings, 2 to 3 feet................. 150

Spirea Anthony Waterer, 2 year transplanted..................................... 45

  prunifolia, 2 year transplanted... 50

  thunbergi, 2 year transplanted... 50

  van Houttei, 1 year, 12 to 18 inches... 25

   transplanting grade 17

Weigela hendersonia, 1 year transplanting grade............................... 45

  rosea, 1 year transplanting grade.. 45

CPSIA information can be obtained
at www.ICGtesting.com
Printed in the USA
LVHW011822061118
596180LV00013BA/1006/P